How To Stop Procrastinating

A Comprehensive Guide To Proven Tactics For Conquering Your Inner Procrastinator, Mastering Your Time, And Boosting Your Productivity. Improving Your Productivity In The Quickest Time

Anthony Vithale

HOW TO STOP PROCRASTINATING

Table of Contents

Introduction

A lchemy is an old mystery and secret science. His practicers mainly tried to transform lead into gold, a search which for thousands of years has captured people's imaginations. The aims of alchemy, though, go way beyond merely making golden sticks.

Alchemy was grounded in a deep metaphysical world view, in which everything about us holds a sort of divine energy, and metals were not only assumed to exist, but also to evolve inside the Earth. If a base or common metal such as plumbing is detected, it was deemed merely to be a morally and physically unstable type of higher metals such as gold. For the alchemists, metals were not the special compounds in the periodic table, but the same element at various points of growth or progress on the road to moral excellence.

James Randi states,' Starting around the year 100 and entering his flower in the Middle Ages, alchemy was an art that is focused in a large degree on science and partly on sorcery, as James Randi refers to it's' Encyclopedia of Legends, Frauds, and Hoaxes of the Occult and Supernatural,' Many scientists believe alchemy has its origins in ancient Egypt. China has also arisen as a new center of alchemical thought. Therefore,

Alchemy was a form in chemistry because it occurred around 25 years ago before chemistry was established to us today in the period in Robert Boyle (1627–1697) and Antoine Lavoisier (1743–1784). The alchemy was an early predecessor of chemistry, involving much of the industrial methods known as metals and alloys, the development of gold and gold paints, and the processing and application of pigments, dyes, and therapeutics. Alchemy was often regarded as the industrial arts.

Alchemy exists in its broadest context as a method of science that attempts to explore the nature of creation and to master the production of inanimate substances. The alchemists ' main goals were to transmute base metals into gold and achieve the "Philosopher's Stein," a material that brought beauty to existence. The Elixir Vitae, the Grand Magisterium, and the Crimson Tincture were other examples of the Philosopher's Stone and were called basic medicines.

The gold obsession of alchemy originated from the belief that gold was the ultimate element. When the nature of this precious metal could be understood (the argument went), therefore, the meaning of all matter less good than gold could be understood and thereby contribute to the development of all things, including gold. The Stone of the Philosopher introduced the hope that the quality of gold will somehow be converted into the cycles of life. The Stone of the Philosopher was the material from which base metals could be converted into gold and contribute to greater durability by extrapolation. Ses theories were used in the Chinese alchemists ' introduction to alchemy. We found a liquid gold shape that would encourage immortality, and liquid gold represented the core of the Stone of the Philosopher, and the quest for liquid gold was one path towards the Stone of the Philosopher. The Chinese alchemists were involved in the processing of artificial cinnabar, which they claimed to be the red "life-giving pigment." They also became involved in transmuting base metals into gold. The emphasis of alchemical thinking and method was thus the alteration of matter to improve lifespan eventually.

First Chapter

Alchemy is not a superstition, but it often occurs in the supernatural and is used to promote spiritual growth. It indicates you are gaining control over existence. Power is the alchemy's center. It is understandable that alchemy is spiritual and mystical metaphor which originated from early Western chemistry. When you follow the direction of the alchemists, that will show you the highest stages of sorcery.

We all equate alchemy with the medieval practice of making ordinary objects even more valuable; in particular, the production of precious gold and silver from simple base metals, and the discovery of panacea by the alchemist or' Elixir of Life.' The definition of alchemy is older men in a laboratory who combine metals, but it's far more than that.

Many people equate sorcery with alchemy. Isaac Newton, the renowned father of science, was an alchemist. At the moment, alchemy was unlawful since alchemists might falsify the coins of this period. The job of many alchemists was then to identify the right materials for building a foundation for philosophers. This material is a mystical one that can be used to preserve existence, heal cancer, transform crystal into gems and convert metals into gold. There have been several articles about how to build the stone of the philosopher.

Trojanis cited the transmutation gave time and place. The explanation provided is that alchemical processes do not take place at the usual table but around time, energy and space itself. All and all, alchemy is a time travel and a mystical path. In 1915 the Rosicrucian or emder's founder Harvey Spencer Lewis reportedly turned zinc into gold using a large open fire and a crucible. The latest documents documenting the general public show have been regularly released in a variety of business publications.

Alchemy was given several abstract meanings; in Jungian philosophy, the mechanism signifies an person's quest for oneself and the transmutation of "human" alternatives. This path begins in the unconscious, progresses into the division of the mind into different elements. The four stages of development are depicted by different colors: Black equating to the primordial, guilty, first, white Mercury symbolic, feminine and rapid silver, red meaning man, sulfur and desire, and gold (lapis) the total synthesis and transcendence.

Seven operations are recognized: calcination (death of profane), rottenness (cause of calcination and division of the destructed remains) solution (purification of matter) distillation (of elements of redemption from previous operations), relation (joining parallels, Jung's closer union), sublimation (suffering as the result of spiritual detachment a a There are seven identifiable operations:

Second Chapter

Alchemy is central to Jung's common unconscious theory. This book begins with an overview of the process and the goals of Jung's psychotherapy. It then develops the above analogies and its own understanding of the analytical process.

Jung remembers the simultaneous ity of alchemy, which involves both the chemical phase and the magical dimension counterpart. We also speaks of the alchemists ' seemingly intentional mystification.

Finally, Jung stresses the significance of alchemy for us in regards to the transcendent essence of the mind by utilizing the alchemical cycle to offer insights into individualization.

Jung claims that the meaning of alchemy is closely connected to the psychoanalytical method. Through one of his patients ' vision cycles he explains how the objects utilized by the alchemists appear in their psyches as part of the mythological representations that the man creates in his dreams. Jung makes an parallel between the Brilliant Work of the Alchemists and the reintegration and social individualization of the current clinical patient.

In making these comparisons Jung emphasizes the fundamental essence of his model philosophy and provides an impassioned case for the value of faith in the common man's mental wellbeing. Another illustration of Jung's tremendous erudition and obsession of mystical and exoteric manifestations of faith and psyches of theology and mysticism is demonstrated through vividly detailed pictures, sketches and paintings from alchemy and other mythological myths like Christianity.

Psychology is a crucial endeavor to revalue a network of lost thoughts and has led greatly to the resurgence of Alchemy as a serious force in western metaphysical and occult culture. Inspired by seminal research by Ethan Allen Hitchcock and Herbert Silberer (who was in effect inspired by Jung).

It is also fascinating regarding this book to learn that scientist Wolfgang Pauli, who will collaborate with Jung on theories like the acausal connection theory of synchronicity, is the patient whose dreams were discussed in the second part. The hallucinations are viewed as a sequence to explain the significances of repeated motivations and images, with the sequence resulting in a' universal clock,' which simply comprises of many clocks on different plane sizes and colors, as a result of Pauli's latent anticipation of a great celestial order. Jung also listed three of the strongest of these visions in his Terry lectures on religious psychology.

The fundamental theory That is advancing about the relationship between alchemy and psychology is that there is no strong differentiation between object and topic among pre science people and this causes them unconsciously to project their own inner states on external artifacts (especially artifacts that are still unknown to them). Without this rational distinction of perception, the universe became phenomenologically entirely different, because individuals could not discriminate between the characteristics of the entity they viewed and their own ideals, feelings and convictions. This is partially why the Alchemists can not know precisely what the philosopher's stone actually is and that the product has so many distinct symbols.

Gold, compounds are classified in the way the alchemist attempts to grasp matter and to produce base metals in their purest form depending on their expected importance. The Jung Documents as such alchemists jointly realize that they themselves must reflect the changes they aim to create inside their materials: for example, if they intend to attain the philosopher's stone which can save' foundation' or' vulgar' metals, the alchemist must therefore become a redemptive person. The alchemists understood that they wanted to redempt nature like Christ had redempted the individual, hence their association with Christ the Redeemer. Through this view, the Opus (work) of alchemy is a conceptual account of the basic cycle undergone by the human mind as it reorients the belief structure and generates significance through chaos. This opus begins with the nigredo (blackening, analogous to despair and nihilistic loss of value) to return to the exploiting raw material and to go into a cycle of metaphysical purification which will reconcile appearingly irreconcilable opposites (Coniunctio) in order to achieve new stages of consciousness.

Religious and Psychological Problems of Alchemy

Jung's core theory is that Alchemy relies on a broad variety of signals, pictures and symbols from the West's Mutual Unconsciousness. Jung supports his study of the mind and spirit against numerous opponents who, based on their point of view, accused him of being atheist and anti-religious. He promotes a greater interpretation of Western cultural practices, for example. Esoteric Christianity and alchemy, along with an Western review, for example. Buddhism, Hinduism among others. Jung recognizes Western moral tranquility of not fully accepting the Christian ideology as a course to transition. Alchemy, he claims, is a' Modern Meditation' intended to make things simpler. The book begins with a summary of a whole set of dreams mentioned by an anonymous individual (to protect confidentiality), which Jung interprets in its archetypal and mythological context. This attempts to demonstrate Jung's collective unconscious philosophy, and his philosophical purpose, or his great research in social and moral unification or dignity via the cycle in individualisation. Which affects the condition of the mind.

Individual Dream Symbolism in Alchemy

Jung's main idea is that Alchemy depends on a broad range of Western Unconscious signs, pictures and symbols. Jung defends his analysis of the mind and spirit of various detractors who suspected him of being atheistic andanti-religious based on their belief. For eg, it encourages a greater awareness of Western cultural activities.Esoteric Christianity and alchemy along with, for starters, a Western study.Buddhism, among others Hinduism.

Jung accepts Western spiritual peace that Christian philosophy is not universally embraced as a path of change. He says that alchemy is a' simple therapy' to clarify issues. The book starts with a description of a whole sequence of dreaming, which Jung interprets in his archetypal and mythological sense, described by an unidentified person (to preserve confidentiality).

This attempts to demonstrate Jung's common unconscious ideology and his metaphysical aim or his thorough work into social and moral unity or honesty via an human process. This influences the mind's state.

Key Concepts in Alchemy

I. Hermeticism (AKA "Hermetism")

We posed the query concerning alchemy before —"Was it a faith, a science, or something else?"YetHermeticism may be told the same. We should call it a theology since it is named the "PriscaTheologia" by its adherents (that Hermetizism is one valid theology that runs across all religions and that it has been provided specifically by God to ancient man)).

Hermetism is based on the doctrines of mystic Hermes Trismegistus, a character whose past is as misterful as the religion he was initiating: is Hermes Trismegistus a human man, a deity, a mixture of heaven + man, a mixture of many gods (these include the Greek god Hermes and the Egyptian heaven Thoth)?

There is no solution to this problem because we do not know when Hermes Trismegistus existed (some argue that he was a contemporary or even a tutor of Abraham the Jewish Patriarch which, if real, would date him around 2500 years before Christ).

In light of these complexities, let's concentrate on Hermes Trismegistus ' instruction, which are the foundations of hermetic theology. Hermeticism is an immense expanse of understanding, but for our sakes we shall expand on this overarching definition...' There is a transcendent Deity, or an Absolute, of which we and the entire world partake' and that man should learn how to purify the divine (and thereby himself) in such a way that he becomes one with' Everything:

a. The Emerald Tablet: (AKA "Tabula Smaragdina") reported to be the source of the philosophical phrase "As Above, So Below..."

The Emerald Tablet reads:

Tis true without lying, certain & most true.

The one below is like the one above and the one above is like the one below to do the wonders in one aspect only. Just because all things have become just evolved from one, from one's meditation: so all things have their roots from this one aspect, through adaptation.

The Sun is her parent, the moon is her mum, the wind carries her in her belly; the earth is her nurse.

The creator of all excellence is here all over the globe.

A energy or force is full until it is transformed into rock.

Divide the planet from oil, the delicate from the major industry sweetly.

It rises from earth to heaven and then it goes back to earth and absorbs the energy of higher and lower things.

You will have the riches of the entire universe, and the evil will flee from you.

The power is above all the energy. Any delicate aspect is overcome and a powerful element penetrates.

So the world was created.

This is why the means (or process) herein are exemplary adaptations. Therefore, I am called Hermes Trismegist, because all three pieces of the universe theory that I have mentioned regarding the process of the Sun is finished and concluded.

b. Corpus Hermeticum

The holy 18 chapter text of the Hermetic Religion is meant to record the conversation between God and Hermes, through which God express His knowledge with Hermes, who then shares it with His disciples.

c. The 3 Parts of the Wisdom of the Universe

A hermetic practitioner seeks to learn how to perfect 3 "crafts." These are:

The Craft of Alchemy (the operation of the Sun).

The Craft of Astrology (the operation of the Stars).

The Craft of Theurgy (the operation of the gods AKA 'magic').

The mastery of these three crafts was meant to supply the hermetic with all the knowledge of the world, which, when understood, would unlock the way for a person to achieve a higher consciousness, and finally find communion with the Divine.

It is the main goal of The Great Project (see below).

Interesting Note: We learn that John used The Emerald tablet in John's last Temptation, but not anything is mentioned regarding Hermes Trimegistus, the corpus hermeticum, or the knowledge of the world.

II. The 3 Alchemic Agents

1. The Philosopher's Stone

There is perhaps no more common idea of alchemy (and misunderstood) than the famous Stone Philosopher—the mysterious material?) (is believed to transform lead into gold.

It was obtained by heating the essential metals in a pear-shaped glass collapse (AKA The Philosopher's Egg, Hermetic tube). Because the phase involves the base materials, the colour changed: "black signaling the death of the old material preparatory for revitalization; white, the color needed to be turned into silver; and red, the highest level, the color appropriate to become gold."

Imagine for yourself... The Philosopher's Stone, sometimes named The Stone of the Philosopher, The Materia prima, The White Stone by the water, The Magisterium, The Stone of the

Learned, The Diamond of Perfection, and the Sword in the Rock. This is possible that the Philosopher's stone was the most prominent because of its supposed role of turning BASE metals (lead, iron, zinc, copper, mercury) into PRECIOUS metals (silver and gold), at least as the alchemists claimed.

Note, many alchemists (especially in Europe in the Middle Ages), under the overt gaze of the Catholic Church performed their art.

Once the continually starving for wealth church was informed that they should one day sell endless quantities of silver and gold, alchemists should follow their studies (and concealed their actual real purpose to use The Stone).

Most people still believe that the true intent of the Stone of the Philosopher was.

a. Create the Elixir of Life to achieve immortality.

b. Obtain Perfection of The Self – AKA Complete Enlightenment and heavenly bliss as part of The Magnum Opus (see below).

c. To obtain the Knowledge of Creation – i.e. man's final inner transformation (of his "base" self) into his higher (precious or divine) self.

2. *Alkahest vs Azoth*

Although it is often assumed to be the same thing, a deeper analysis reveals that Alkahest and Azoth are clearly very distinct alchemical agents.

Alkahest

Alkahest was the alchemical' absolute solvent.' Alkahest's aim was to sell every other material–like gold.

Paracelsus (legend suggests that Paracelsus came up with the word alkaest and is supposed to have originally been the philosopher's stone) and his brother FranciscusMercurius Van Helmont (who created a principle of Liquor Alkahest) were the key contributors to the creation of alkaest in alchemies.

The obstacle to create an alkahest was that the most models were such potent solvents that they appeared to melt anything– a problem... at least for amateurs.

The mystery that is concerning alkahest (and it is maybe the real secret to the higher aims of alchemy) is: the only "absolute" solvent is believed to be waver (since it can remove everything from the simple type over time) from a chemical point of view, and from a mystical point of view there is an alkachest (a material only understood to the alchemy masters) which can remove the body's ailments and del

Azoth

Not to be confused for Alkahest, Azoth is simply quite distinct. While all of them have been stated to be universal drugs, the mechanism by which they have accomplished this goal is critical to their perception of differences. Whereas Alkahest was the predominant SOLVENT, the alternative SOLVENT was the azote.

Azoth (nee Azoc) is strongly connected with mercury (a primary alchemy of the old alchemists to be the "animating force concealed in all that makes for transmutation").

A description of azote deepens even further than alkahest of metaphysics. As the latter, azote is related to the Stone Theory and the Elixir of Existence but, unlike alkahest, azote has a far richer past (dating back to the early alchemists such as Zosimos of Panopolis and Mary the Prophetess).

Currently, Azoth is aligned with all these higher alchemical goals:

a. The Kaballah principle of Shamayim, which is "the first flood of the Word of God," and is "the Blood of the Soul." Edem (the steaming substance or mist) becomes "the immaterial dust with which God created Adam." It renders the nature of soul azoth.

b. Azoth is not only thought to be "the body's animating force (spirit animatus), but also the intellectual strength and excitement."

c. Azoth is claimed by some to be "the nature or mind of God."

3. *Elixir Vitae*

As we spend a lot of time discussing related subjects, we should be short. As you already know, alchemists across the globe were continuously trying to find a material which would give them everlasting life or immortality–this was the famed Elixir Vitae (AKA. The Elixir of Life).

Throughout China, alchemists have blended and eaten various elixirs made of jade, cinnabar, hematite, and gold. While one of them does not know whether immortality has been accomplished, we realize that many have died of Chinese poisoning alchemical elixir–yikes!

Alchemists in India concentrated on discovering the elixir they named Amrita from the nectar of gods. The approach of seeking Amrita differed based on the kind of faith (Hindu, Christianity, Sikhism, etc).

In Europe, the search for the development of an Elixir Vitae became an important part of the usage of the Stone of the Philosophers.

We don't know if all of them find their Holy Grail.

A Paradox? In the Last Temptation of John's novels, Christ made John's main character eternal. During his long life, John turned to alchemy frequently to find answers for Existence when world religions did not perform this mission. While John has also been an alchemy master, Elixir of Life—if anything, John has asked for the Elixir of Death—is one thing the ship will never bring to him!

III. The 14 Keys of Alchemy

The English alchemist Samuel Norton worked in the 1500's. His studies include the 14 guide to Alchemy, which explains the mechanisms by which the alchemicals travel from the moment they are first inserted into a test tube until they are ready to be harvested / used in higher-level alchemical experiments. In 1577, this list was written.

Solution, the transition from a gaseous or stable state to equilibrium.

Filtration, the mechanical removal of the residual objects from the material trapped in it.

Evaporation, transition or transfer by heat from a liquid or solid state into a vaporous state.

Distillation, an action that distinguishes a sticky material from the compounds in solution.

Separation, process of compounds disuniting or decomposing.

Rectification, extraction or purification of any material by repeated distillation.

Calcination, transforming the reactive material from a matter to a powder or calx by thermal operation.

Blending, combining of different ingredients in new compounds or storage. Purification (through putrefaction), accidental disintegration; chemical decay.

Inhibition, preservation or restriction operation. Fermentation, modification of organic ingredients in the presence of a ferment into new compounds.

Fixation, the act or cycle of being dynamic and firm; condition of becoming set.

Multiplying, multiplying or through the act or operation, multiplying the body. The method of turning the base metals into gold.

John's research with the Magnus Opum takes place after these phases in the Last Temptation Sequence, introducing more stages to combine (see Magnus Opum below).

IV. The Magnus Opus – The Great Work

Through alchemy, all that contributes to the completion of the Great Project and the loss of Matter. Throughout the ages, the

Magnus Opum proved to be distinct from other alchemists around the globe... so we are led to believe.

Others suggested that it was part of the transformation of base metals into precious metals by means of the previously mentioned Philosopher's Stone.

The Magnum Opus was believed by some (especially the ones in Hermetic traditions) to be the last step of turning oneself into the Divine.

In a more abstract way, their Magnus Opum put forth true individualism, which was' fulfiling one's destiny in the course of one's creation,' from being a pawn in the hands of destiny to being deliberately appropriate in fulfilling one's own destiny.' Whatever the aims for the Magnus Opum, most texts seem to believe that the phases of the Great Work involved

Third Chapter

Alchemical process and its phases. The "solve et coagula" principle and the 4 phases: Nigredo(black phase), Albedo (white phase), Citrinitas(yellow phase) and Rubedo (red phase) and their connections with the 4 elements, Ground ,Water, Air and Fire.

Process that involves burning the material at very high temperatures to see if something survives the fire. Evaporation of waste substances. If something survives, it is called "alchemical lead", a raw substance that can be worked through many steps to transmute into "alchemical gold".

Alchemical Process of Transformation

Understanding Transmutation as the Basis of Alchemy.

Alchemy is well recognized as it assumes that lead can be turned into gold. Nevertheless, the transmutation of non-precious metals into gold is merely a symbol for the soul to be released from its "empty leading existence," to know its own lightness and pure spirit.

The alchemists felt that the foundation of the natural universe was the prime matter, or disorderly matter, which could be done if influenced by the shape. "Forms" appeared in the shape of the atoms, of soil, of water, of fire, and of the air. The Alchemists deduced from the combination of elements in particular, that the infinite varieties of existence are formed.

The four components were characterized by four characteristics of fluidity, dryness, heat and cold. Every factor has two of these fundamental qualities. The four possible variations are therefore:

- hot + dry --> fire;
- hot + fluid (or moist) --> air;
- cold + fluid --> water;
- cold + dry --> earth

One of the two qualities predominates in each element. In earth, dryness; in water, cold; in air,

fluidity; in fire, heat.

Therefore, transmutation is feasible. Each item may be converted into another through the content they exchange. Therefore fire will become air via the heat system, much as air through fluidity process can become gas.

By eliminating one component from each one, two components may also become a third element. Fire and water may become air by dividing with the dry and cold qualities; with the warm and fluid properties, the same elements will contribute to earth.

Consider the basic illustration of the transmutation cycle in which a slice of green wood is heated.

Drops of water appear at the split end of the log, therefore wood contains water; vapors and steam is then emitted and wood contains air; wood then burns and reveals that only ash remains we know that the wood contains dirt.

Alchemists treated certain materials in the same manner, especially metals, i.e. a metal owes its unique shape to the particular proportioning of the four elements.

The psychological conditions and issues that clients still present today demonstrate the existence of elements but in skewed proportions; for example, an over-stressed mind may alchemically be represented as excess fire (hot and dry). It attempts to intervene with water escape (tears) and relieves the overheated mind that will then "cool down." But, our can intervene more frequently than not and we obstruct our tears and therefore the tension rises.

The sulphur-mercury hypothesis was a related idea stemming from the four elements principle.

This principle incorporated in a different way the two contrasting or opposite components, fire and water. The first was rendered of the primary qualities of heat and warm, the second with the primary qualities with cold and damp. Heat was "sulphur" and water "mercury." Sulfur was usually the property of combustibility or the fire spirit, and mercury was the property of fusibility or the metal mineral spirit.

As sulfur and mercury joined to varying quantities and degrees of pureness, according to the principle of sulfur-mercury the various metals and minerals took form. If sulfur and mercury were completely pure, the result would be the best element, namely gold, if mixed into the most full equilibrium.

The creation of silver, cherry, lead, iron or copper was attributable to flaws in purity and, in fact, in proportion. Nevertheless, because these lower metals were actually composed with the same elements as gold, the mixture occurrence may be resolved by effective treatment and elixirs.

We don't have to take a view on the physical world from medieval alchemists, but instead, we can derive two essential a priori postulates, the foundations of alchemical logic, by metaphorical interpretation:

The essence of existence embodied by the concept of the primitive substance by which all beings were created and through which they could be discarded once more.

The presence of a strong transmuting agent that can facilitate the transition of one kind of substance into another. This fictional entity was known as the "rock of the philosopher," the best known of all alchemical theories.

If we consider the prima materia, the initial state of existence, as the true, real, raw state of consciousness from which all consciousnesses, i.e. rocks, plants, creatures, and humans, originated, and if we consider the philosopher's stone as an evolved state of consciousness when we are on the earthly body, the two concept above is relevant to our psychotherapy practice.

Still, aside from a handful of the more learned alchemists of medieval times, more practitioners felt that they would turn lead into gold literally.

The literature reveals that the disgruntled gold-makers were interwoven with a subterranean maze of delusions, nightmares, illusions and dreams.

Therefore, what seemed to be the worst error for the bulk of "alchemical hopefuls" was their greatest achievement: the "sons of Hermes" had found, in the silence of the blind lane, the unconscious by their enabled imagination.

Carl Jung noted that much of the visions and observations that his patients made strikingly corresponded to the explanations described in alchemical texts. Jung also believed that alchemy awareness could be viewed as an tool for use in psychotherapy to grasp the mechanism of psychological and spiritual change.

Projection and Unconscious Imagery in Alchemy

Alchemist's research was sluggish and laborious in which free thinking, hallucinations and perceptions of the unconscious took place not just in his thoughts, but also as he gazed in his furnaces and experimented with his tools.

A variety of explanations follow: Hoghelande informs us: "They inform us that various titles are assigned to the stone because of the marvelous variation of figures that occur during research, as colors sometimes emerge at the same moment, while we often picture strange animal forms, snakes or trees in the clouds or in the sun.

From the 12th century when the Arabs initiated it, to the 16th, when the alchemist laboratories became psychological laboratories and the alchemical research became inquiries into the inner world, the art of alchemy shifted dramatically throughout Europe. The purgations and regeneration of metals have been transformed into abstract cycles of purging and changing the spirits.

The encounter between the alchemists and the Unconscious, therefore, had a transformative influence on the alchemical practice and started to evolve by the end of the Middle Ages into a systemized magical transforming method known as the opus alchymicum. Yet, with the advent of the human spirit in the 17th century, chemistry theory demolished basic principles and alchemy ideas and substituted them with an analytical structure, from which our chemistry education evolved.

It was only in the 20th century, and with the growth of deep psychology that the road was opened for the reemergence of Alchemy and for it to assume its place as a center of information that could educate and impact psychotherapy education and practice.

The Contribution of Alchemy to Modern Psychotherapy

Recent theories in alchemy, Jung's most notable being "Psychology and Alchemy," have transformed our minds. In 1946, his research on the "Psychology of the Transference Interpreted with a variety of Alchemical Illustrations" showed a specific light on the transition of psychotherapy that was primarily inspired by the works of Sigmund Freud until the time of this release, namely that the transmitting of knowledge was merely a process which was a result of the connection between parent and infant. Instead, Jung's research on alchemy revealed that his customers ' transition dreams and interactions centered primarily on an inner individualization phase.

This approach acknowledges, of course, the value of the experience of connecting with and separation from the parent, but it goes beyond that by considering existence as a continuing growth phase. The clients ' expectations on the psychiatrist thus represent some of their own inner psychological universe instead of Freud's perception that the client is simply a father.

Alchemy's greatest contribution to psychotherapy is the interpretation of the development process. This is important, on the one side, to the basic method of improving the way we look at the universe and, on the other side, to an awareness of the divine change phase. The texts "Alchemical Studies" (1931– 54) and "The MysteriumConiunctionis" (1956) by Jung are historical research on language and transition cycles.

The Stages of Transformation

According to the text read, the alchemical cycle of transformation has been defined in a variety of ways as a 6-stage phase, 12 stages, 20, 22, 50, and even 75 stages!

However, the alchemical cycle can be interpreted in four essential steps, which are most helpful when beginning as an "alchemical novice" and when attempting to link it to the psychotherapy.

The "Four Stage" Version

The process can be represented as nigredo, albedo, citrinitas, and rubedo in four stages.

At each stage, the alchemist is subjected to an ever more rigorous purification, accompanied by a combination with the fire (alchemical marriage), a resurrection of a new sense of self, and then the death of that sense of self (to progress to the next level).

The fire is twice as powerful at each point as the previous burn. The fire may also be seen as a four degrees fiery love to awaken in the alchemist's heart, either through his anima or "inner woman soul mate" (in the case a man) or through his animus or "inner woman's spirit."

In alchemy, both the anima (in men) and the animus (in women) go through four phases of creation, which in effect relate to the four phases of the alchemical union. At every point, the perception of this "fiery love" purifies and awakens the Alchemist to make him/her more conscious of himself and to make his / her heart more guarded. Fire is both the fuel for alchemical research and the key agent in the continuous transmutation cycle. When learned, the fire of the alchemist is sustained without interruption before the cycle is completed.

Stage One: Nigredo or "Blackening."

At the first stage, the fire is sluggish and soft, as if from the flesh or the embryo, and slowly progresses to the first step of the job, resulting in the earthly nigredo or blackening.

The research starts with a quest for "prima content," which the alchemists invented as a requirement for reflecting the initial, pure and uncorrupted state of affairs that constitute the foundation of existence, i.e., the elements arising from prima matter. They also recognized that all existence is restored after death and that an individual must first die in order to evolve.

For e.g., an apple will putrefy until its seed can take root and create more apples. Naturally, this "putrefaction" not only refers to the natural universe but also to the metaphysical realm as material death is needed to bring things about, so spiritual death is necessary for the spiritual renaissance of man.

So, the much sought after an act of renaissance is always preceded by a return to the source of life-depends on a "reduction to the primal material," and the fire is a key element in achieving this.

From a conceptual point of view, this stage reaches a deep, turbulent inner universe. St. John of the Cross refers to this as the first of two dark days, the dark night of the soul, which is an encounter of the darkest elements of our own selves. At first, nothing makes sense, in reality, what the psychiatrist can do at this point of the cycle is engage entirely and empathize with the person who encourages it more through the articulation of his/her encounter.

The psychological atmosphere, i.e., the counseling region, becomes the hermetically sealed tank, and the internal chaos in which the person joins symbolizes the responses of enemies that fight against each other. It ensures that the subconscious of the client shows to the waking mind the unconscious inner struggles. When the person starts seeing the inner environment more emotionally, the cycle intensifies (increases in the fire), and sometimes rage, anxiety, and disappointment are expressed and an urge to "break from it all."

It takes patience, humility and acceptance not just from the client but also from the therapist who knows from experience that the purification process is ongoing and that one by one, the inner conflicts are gradually settled until a completely new interior condition of clarity and freedom is reached. Therefore, the user will be reconciled to the essence of his own world-they will have merged with his' earth spirit' alchemically. During the first level, interaction with earth nature requires that the sense of self be released from its association with the elements of land and water. Everything we're seeking to do is through the veils of implicit connection to the universe and make things easier that we are on this planet.

I am not, for example, my relatives, my work, nor my rank, which people remember worldwide. Our relation to worldly objects (their bodies, the material things, parent figures, etc.) is the way we interact with the earth dimension. And although we remain attached to worldly things, we remain divided and segregated throughout. When we break the bonds, we will transform inward to pursue our inner guide and animus, through which we awaken the fire (and later love), which contributes to the first alchemical marriage or union.

The water dimension symbolizes the emotions we feel when we meet and break these attachments—anxiety, rage, sorrow, etc. —emotions that we need to undergo to detach them and therefore pass on to the next level. Therefore, as the implicit essence of the world in us first comes to light, we immediately experience pessimistic thoughts and emotions.

When we have surmounted the implicit identifications, emotions and perceptions are constructive, that is, the universe no longer menacs our true self, because we are free of them and can determine when and how we incorporate the environment into ourselves (rather than getting engulfed into ourselves and discarded into the universe). Once we join the unconscious, we also sense these feelings as water pictures such as the sea or a lake or river. This is also a sign that we continue to "float with" our internal cycle, indicating that we have let go of our connection to the stable outer world (earth element) and obey our feelings.

The successful experience with our inner anima (for men) or inner animus (for women is a symbol of operating beyond these worldly associations and their accompanying emotions. The alliance, or "marriage with earth nature," has been accomplished when the actual alliance with the inner anima or animus is felt. The anima is symbolized by the focus of sensual love Eve at this point. The animus is symbolized by the physical image of "Tarzan." This union paves the way for the unconscious power of existence on earth to become open. The alchemists view the very act of becoming free of this existence as awakening through the sublimation of the air dimension contributing to the liberation of the soul form.

The first disclosure of the essence of the spirit is followed by childlike visuals in consumer visions. It marks the first self-renaissance. For women, the vision of regeneration is sometimes accompanied by pregnancy dreams.

Completion of the first step is now perceived as a burial, in effect, a complete letting go of the ancient sense of self instinctively associated with existence on earth. Fire and fire pictures also surround flame and destruction images. We are now ready to enter stage two. We explain so far the union of opposites (alchemical marriage), the new self's rebirth, and the old ones demise. Purification has also been a continuous part of the operation, primarily via the fire aspect.

Stage Two: Albedo or "Whitening."

And like the first step is considered the terrestrial gathering, so the second period is named the lunar step.

This calls for additional purification of our psyche and receptiveness to the nature of our souls, who originally came into existence without any worldly experiences, family, environment, and society.

Awareness of our own identity is the first true move in addressing the query' who am I?' Alchemical scriptures talk about the owner becoming aware of its own inner existence—an inner reflecting in, symbolized by the moon, finding a pure essence, a source of life and energy. It is this "force," also known as the "waters of creation," that allows the neophyte to overcome the limits of the mind and to reach the angelic limits.

In the psychotherapeutic sense, this is a time of a little isolation from reality, only participatory enough to hold it "running through," with the major powers within. This causes consumers to remember themselves instantly and therefore continue to doubt their way of life. During a moment of clarity, it becomes simpler to see what is important and what is not. Alchemists often refer to this as "sublimation," analogous to the vapors flowing from the chemical vessel under boiling, which holds the substance searched for and is to be removed. This is a symbol for the spirit, which emerges from the depths of the rich mind and eventually discovers the retrieval of the essence of the spirit. At this level, it knows who you are as an independent person and what your strengths and talents are. This duration contributes to enhanced personal knowledge and intent for those who fully, profoundly, and persistently follow their rehabilitation cycle.

And though alchemists identify the fire from stage two as "low and mild, as from the June Sun," it is considerably more extreme than the previous level. Throughout life, we are then faced with the need to be far more scrupulous, accessible, courageous, and racist. The road becomes solitary when we move inward, but the cycle takes tremendous honesty, courage, and determination to succeed.

Like the first stage of the cycle, the second alchemical marriage is achieved. Here the moon lady, an object of romantic affection, fits the image of the anima.

This is the purpose of Eros, not anatomy, as Helen of Troy is a classic example. The animus character in question (for women) is the loving hero, the poet (Byron), the movie star (Harrison Ford), author (Ernest Hemingway), adventurer, cultural liberator, etc. After the inner union, a second "lunar boy" rebirth takes place. The baby boy, representing the freshly acquired state of consciousness, is particularly delicate and vulnerable, indicating the solely responsive condition achieved by the consciousness. The sense of existence now understands the essence of the mind.

Stage Three: Citrinitas or "Yellowing."

Alchemists refer to Citrinitas as the sun's level or the dawning of our being's "solar light." Today, like in the moon or spirit sun, the sun is no longer reflectionary. The essence is clear, and it is ubiquitous (we don't believe it has a source). This light is "powerful and intense as a calcinating spark." It is often referred to as the initial light or as the pure and imaginative perception of light. Many alchemical texts identify it as the Divine Intellect (separate from the human mind). The only real information is supposed to be known to us as this Light is aware of us.

Now, in discussing the second step, only an alchemical marriage and a rebirth were stated. Step 3 ends with "yellow death," i.e., a dying of the "luminous sun" to the extent where it is simply "black night," a sun which is as vivid as our inner sight is obscured and seems to be darkness. St. John of the Cross speaks about this in a detailed description of his own

"Dark Night of the Soul." From the Buddhist point of view, this "death" was often represented as a loss of the illusion that one is a different entity. It is a total death of the dualistic state of mind, which treats both subject and object as distinct.

The comparable background of psychotherapeutic settings is challenging to locate, but we have an indication if we take schizophrenic behavior into consideration. There, the consumer will lose their sense of identity and step into an environment that is almost completely empirical, and that has little to little capacity to be impartial, i. e. to distinguish the client from the interaction.

The "Yellow Death" signals the termination of the power of "lunar illumination." This "solar illumination" awakens the feeling of discovery and unveiling awareness, and the mind is transformed into the "solar sun." Internal awareness is not achieved by research, meditation, or reflective thought; it must be perceived as a clear realization.

Further explanations of this stage are too abstract to be important, and we must, therefore, continue with the third alchemical marriage explanation.

At this level, purification focuses on the elimination of the "watery" components. The animal image, or divine woman, as the focus of spiritual affection, is unveiled in this alchemical union. Such passion is fundamentally devotional. One result will be Dante's Beatrice, who takes the author to the realms of divine passion and paradise.

The accompanying animus character acts as the divine advisor–the educator, clergyman, priest, who is shown as being "strong and spiritualized." Rebirth is a revelatory sun, in reference to the emergence of the solar consciousness.

Because stage three has evidently progressed through the spiritual realms, continuing to search for references from the psychotherapeutic sense that offer us an indication of this activity-it is maybe better left, i.e., as a supernatural encounter-may seem futile.

Yet the unconscious awareness we sometimes gain in reality, in a vision or in a burst of understanding, offers us at least some indication of the "revelatory sun" or solar energy force. It is possible that there is a stage in the healing cycle through which a single thought, insight, or picture that comes to us may be a definitive turning point or sum up the entirety of a therapy

Through this way, we may conclude that our insight applies to the universal metaphysical wisdom that is already understood at this point.

This was historically referred to as mere intellect. Obviously, we do not recognize where the insight stems from, or whether it "knows" and nor are we expected to feel this "mystical illumination" through counseling. To know much about this point, we have to focus on the illuminations of those exceptional few people who have documented their experiences.

Stage Four: Rubedo or "Reddening".

In stage four, the alchemist wakes up to the need to return to earth to truly embrace his condition of "enlightened" awareness in the mind and body. To order to do that, the fourth purifying heat, "hot and fiery as combustion," must be added to create fresh coagulation of spirit and matter.

The conclusion of step three leaves the alchemist fully drained of pure energy, pure intellect, space, time, and shape, but without a body or mind consciousness.

So the destruction of' red mortalities' at the beginning of stage four means the demise of the liberation found in this process and the dissolution, as human soul desiring to be incarnated without a sense of alienation from its original pure mind, of the aware existence of pure spirit (and pure intelligence).

And after the soul is fully reflected in the mind/body (psyche) will the condition of divine fullness be understood. Heaven and planet are now joined in the alchemist.

In fact, the cycle becomes unfinished and potentially dysfunctional at the completion of phase three, and as a mechanism to incarnate, no organism or soul is there, and the mind/organism must ultimately suffer from regression into its initial impure, leading condition.

However, Spirit is not supposed to incarnate into the old (loaded) state of mind/body because, if that occurs, there will be little reason, i.e., the soul will be returning to its leading position, or worst yet, removed from the ego, and leaving the alchemist in an internal separation.

The psyche has to be reawakened — "materially spiritualized" is the word used— such that the soul will incarnate into a fitting body; that is, the psyche now can convey the attributes and essence of the soul as the psyche is similar to the soul.

This relation between the spirit/soul and the mind/body forms the final and most essential alchemical union. Then the anima is the Goddess of Christ, an item of divine devotion, a consort of Christ.

The animus people involved are the Enlightened People— Jesus, Buddha, Saints, etc.

All it implies is that through being born into the earth's universe, God's consciousness actively recognizes its God-like essence-as a holy, transcendental entity and in communion with the universal whole.

It, therefore, is the stone of the philosopher which the alchemist tried. This is the final culmination of the Final Job.

The psychotherapeutic counterpart is much simpler to grasp, describe, and appreciate than the nuanced mysticism of stage 3.

Clearly stated, after the consumer has understood and transcended the essence of the issues or dilemmas, they have to bring it into action. It requires a shift in their attitude that adapts and embraces their understanding. So, the consumer who discovers that his or her life is a disgrace that has created several issues now starts the path to bring things more in accordance with his or her true nature.

Fourth Chapter

B ring all this back to the inner process that takes place and can happen in a person. Traumas and complexes such as alchemical lead, all attitudes that serve to mask these traumas and complexes (in psychology called "compensations") as waste substances, personal crises of any kind such as alchemical ire that brings out the lead that people they tend not to want to see and hear because they are frightened by all this, the psychoanalytic and internal healing process as an alchemical procedure that transforms a lead into gold.

Personality Types and the Limits of Reason

The beginning of the Great War on 1 August 1914 spared Jung from futile insanity. He considered the awful visitations of his own nightmare until then; now, he realized his fear was premonitorous and transcendent, not to him alone but to Europe's destiny.

Actually calming was the general conflagration. We might believe that it might be alarming to predict such a cataclysm in the past. Nevertheless, Jung appreciated the benefit of a mutual unconscious sensory awareness, such that he did not presume supernatural or diabolical agencies; and his fresh discoveries into the model domain dissipated some of his old fears.

At Symbols of Conversion, he believed that a flowing escape from the common unconscious undoubtedly predicted a catastrophic plunge to unreality, but now he realized that his own recurring visions and delusions gave him a reality.

Schizophrenia was a panicked escape from an untamed mind, frothed, and angry but was unable to bring you any serious damage as long as you did not panic.

Fearlessness allowed him to investigate in detail the unconscious, which he had always believed no scientist might touch, leading him to his most exciting experimental research. What is the term that a scientist would like to refer to his most popular findings sensational? This query encapsulates Jung's ongoing concerns regarding achievement.

Has the heterodox peculiarities of Jung's moral existence, indeed the sheer weirdness, led him to the underlying reality of human nature, or has they kept him in long darkness? Is he the root of real knowledge or a Modern Era charlatan prototype? Which is really the role of research in the creation of its theories? Or what could they sell that might be more important than empirical truth? While he was a ton off, was his instruction a definitive relief for parched soulless modernity?

Jung's scientific perspective, which is often recognized — but yet not always — by traditional psychology and which is common to the ordinary language is the fundamental differentiation between extraverted and introverted personalities, first established in psychological styles (1921).

"When we look at the path of human life, we see that one person's fate is more defined by artifacts of his concern, while another's inner nature is more decided by the issue. Because we are always shrinking further to one hand of the other, we obviously seem to perceive things on our own sort. "Each major category is further subdivided by its prevailing psychological feature, which is that the rational is thought and emotion, whereas the nonrationalis perception and sensation.

This is not to suggest that any entity suits a category and corresponding feature to the exclusion of all else; the structure adapts to countless degrees and distortions of the sort. Not every introvert, even every extravert, includes an introvert. And, through some life-changing events, an introvert may also become an extravert or vice versa.

The following kinds of items reflect the inevitability of human confrontation as it comes to the more important questions: "A guy of his form is so in jail that he can not consider certain views." Workable cultures accept this innate abrasiveness and try everything they can to improve it. Jung firmly opposes systems focused on authoritarian illusions, which can absolutely eradicate these abrasions. "

A man requires a blurry vision, or a rather nebulous perception of human nature to understand the notion that the universal control of existence will guarantee the efficient delivery of happiness... No social rule would ever be able to transcend the psychological gaps between men, the most significant element in the production of the essential energy in the human community. "The best men and women are far-fetched in their own way, for proper comprehension and moral practice, the human race deserves complete morality. The mind is fundamentally unwilling to separate itself from the ego and from a preferably disinterested perch. In pursuit of this right of the narcissistic intellect results ultimately in "paradox and equilibrium."

However, the ego contains all unconscious thoughts, such that it can not be circumscribed by rationality alone. Any other possible psychological activities must be carried out if the quest for the reality is to be successful. The Jungian counselor is far from the mystic, who swears unfailingly.

Jung recognizes his own limits as a thinking introvert— his own category, while someone else may have named him an intellectual introvert. He uses his ideals, he deals with his slips cautiously, and he understands how daunting it is to venture beyond his boundaries. His most esteemed colleagues, each confident in the whole of truth, did not know how their own personalities had formed the major tendencies of their theory: "While the dominant notation in Freudian psychology is a centralist tendency, a struggle for pleasure in the object, Adler wants to be 'on top' to preserve his powder and to strive centrally for the supremacy of the subject.

The Sacred Art of Alchemy and human psychology

In his amazement, C. G. Jung pointed out that the ancient art of alchemy was representing, symbolically, the path which we had all taken embody to our own inherent dignity, what he referred to as the cycle of "individuation." Jung claimed that "I quite soon saw the connection of analytical psychology [Jung's psychology] with alchemy.

In a way, my thoughts were the perceptions of the alchemists, and their environment became my reality. It was a great experience, of course. The alchemists had produced, over the course of centuries, a wide range of symbolic pictures, which directly corresponded to the anatomy of the Unconscious Jung had mapped through his meticulous research with thousands of patients. Jung should himself be called a modern-day alchemist by revealing the nature of the unconscious. Jung adds that "the entire cycle of alchemy... may only be as symbolic of an individual's individualization method." Alchemists have little to little to make a contribution to the chemical industry, least of all the secret of gold-making. Only our excessively one-sided, logical, and intelligent era would ignore this argument so completely and see little in alchemy but an abortive chemistry attempt.

Conversely, the chemistry was a failure and a "loss" to the alchemists, because it required the secularisation and promotion of religious discipline. "Alchemical operations were actual, and this fact was not physical but psychological. Jung points out. Alchemy reflects a laboratory interpretation of a celestial and metaphysical drama. The opus magnum ["great work"] had two goals: the redemption of the human race and that of the world.

The ancient art of alchemy was primarily concerned with turning anything obviously useless to something valuable, converting lead into gold, thereby producing the' philosopher's stone.' However, the "tar" or "lapis" is not a tangible object but is an awakening spirit, which penetrates, forms and gives birth to all things while it appears immaterial. The stone of the philosophers does not only save the particular alchemist; it also affects the area in such a way that it is deemed able to save the whole universe. As Jung emphasizes, the lapis is "a symbolic emblem that represents something produced by humans, but that is superordinate to them." Alchemy is an eternal and holy practice since the purpose of the alchemists is to become a way of having the incarnating god know in time and space.

Alchemy is all about wealth formation. There were thousands of names for alchemical gold and philosophers ' stone, which represented their all-embracing, numinous, mystical properties, which can not be properly defined by the words. Irrespective of its name, the production of the stone is the purpose of the alchemical opus. Alchemy is a magical art form, a real metaphysical quest. "The magical dimension of alchemy is basically a neurological question and is separate from its historical element. It is a concretization of the cycle of individualization in the expected and symbolic manner.

THE PRIMA MATERIA

The "powerful fact," and the foundation of alchemical opera, is the special raw material that is the chaos and raw material that creates a finished substance or "gold." To the alchemists, in the darkness of prima stuff, there was a light, the holy flame hidden in the darkness of substance. Talking about a spirit that is concealed in the matter, Jung clarifies that "the metaphysical counterpart of this concept is the projection of an extraordinarily interesting unconscious substance which, like all these ingredients, reveals a numinous quality-' divine' or' sacrosanct' quality." Symbolically, the mysterious prima matter is the secret material inside us, bearing the unconscious visions. This is the mental emulsion or medium in which the subconscious material is stored inside us. Therefore, prima materia is a sign of the unconscious.

The dark prima matter re-presents and illustrates (through our own inner perceptions, as well as our outer perceptions), our less-developed nature, our the edges, the areas where our interaction with ourselves is not aware. In so far as we unconsciously associate with our unconsciousness, as opposed to being actively associated with it, we shall respond to our unconsciousness, which is the prima materia in practice.

In psychological terminology, we become bloated because, as an individual, we mistakenly associate with the Self (the whole of our being, with both the aware and unconscious elements). Once we are bloated, we behave in the universe, our unconsciousness, and function above our means, outside the boundaries of who we are as individuals. The primitive matter, as an immediate feedback device, would then shift form and represent our unconscious "inflation" not locally, to hold us in check. In its leadlike dimension, the primitive matter includes the essence of despair, a depressive shift into the depths of our being that is perceived as gloomy, which refers to the experience of the moon of psychology. Just like a fantasy balances a unilateral existence, when we become unwittingly bloated, either individually or collectively, the prime matter produces an occurrence that shockes and astounds us to modesty in order to puncture our bind. Once we are bloated, the raw material "grounds" us so that we come grounded to the earth. Perhaps the "crash" isn't going to be too complicated.

It is important to locate the elusive raw material before the opus begins. Psychologically speaking, the enigmatic prima materia reintroduces, is to be uncovered, the parts of the mind we reject, disown and marginalize, the facets of ourselves we are embarrassed of. In Jung's terms, this "means the least we think about, the component that we ignore the most or disregard is just the component comprising the mystery." We generally try to get rid of the shadow of our personalities, but the alchemists realized that our wounded, smaller, and unconscious pieces are not an accident or mistake; they have a meaning. Our wounds, the raw material of the job, are invaluable to the completion of the opus, as the alchemical gold will be no way without these shadow pieces.

Jung said, "and, just as in Christianity, Godhead is concealing in a low-grade guy, so it hides in an awkward stone in' philosophy' [alchemy]." Symbolically speaking, this is the stone' rejected by the founders,' which eventually is the cornerstone. This is an archetypal fundamental concept that the lower is, the higher meaning, that the reward is in the burden, and that we will consider the knowledge in the stupidity. This is an archetypal phenomenon that the greatest meaning-what Jung called the Self and some consider "The Messiah"-is usually contracted and responded to with contempt, anger, resentment, and hatred until remembered for its divinité.

An old alchemical text communicates this notion, stating, "Christ had no shape of comeliness, he was the vilerous of all people, full of griefs and sickness and so scorned that he only veiled the images of him, and he was known as none." The concept that we are to fall into the unconscious, a night-sea voyage, into the depths of our silence, is an archetypal, shamanic one, The first level is the "nigredo," the silence of death, the shadow darker than night, the seed for the eventual creation of the living opus. "The good news announced by the alchemy [analogous to the' Good News' of the Bible] is that, as Jung contemplated, once in Judea a fountain came up, there is now a secret Judea that can not easily be found, and a hidden spring whose water appears unsuited and so bitter that they are considered of no use at all." While potentially lethal, prima material includes its own medication; that is, its own remedy is the alchemical cycle. Prima materia is a mathematical concept since it has an infinite existence with open-ended opportunity, and it includes both poison and medication inside itself.

The more virulent the toxin, the greater the curing ability becomes. Concrete alchemists may transmute the toxin to curing nectar, as when a peacock consumes toxin, the multicolored plumage becomes lightened. Prima Materia is a three-dimensional process that unites dark and light to greater equilibrium. Whether the mercurial and shapeless subject matter actually appears depends on whether we think of it.

"No one has ever understood what this primitive thing is," Jung contemplates. The Alchemists could not, and no one finds out what it really was referred to because it is an abstract material essential for the Incarnation of Christ. "Jung said:" The Alchemists did not know what to write about, definitely not with their intellectual brains, in search of an indescribable spiritual mystery.

The unaware guy, not realizing what they were attempting to say, still passed with the alchemists when it showed itself to him. This describes the sometimes ambiguous, inconsistent, and nonsensical explanation of their work by the alchemists. A lack of integrity and academic rigor has driven the science elite, unnecessarily logical and scientifically challenged, to condemn and denounce alchemy as unscientific and unreasonable nonsense utterly. However, through their denial of alchemy, current physicists of the world condemn the contradictory primary substance within themselves.

Throughout its initial nature, the paradoxical prima matter includes, throughout uncombined, shape the most contradictory opposites found in the human psyche. An explosion of the unconscious, prima materia, as the personification of the instinctual mind, is also symbolized as a dragon!

Prima materia is an uncreated, independent, spirit-like entity that roots in and depends on nothing and is an uncreated, self-generating entity. Jung informs us "It's a right of the Mystical [esoteric, mystery] material to hold' whatever it needs;' a fully independent entity, like the Dragon [uroboros] that engenders, reproduces, destroys and decorates itself... an entity without beginning or end, and in need of no second.

The prima materia is often known as an infant because it is both completely special and entirely original. It's obviously impossible to locate as it's everywhere. The prima materia, as an ancient alchemist cites, is the focus of the "big stone of thinkers, which is still unknown to the entire universe." He clarifies this notion when he states, "the prima materia is universal, it is always and wherever, because it may be projected, always or anywhere."

PROJECTION

Jung brings the crucial point: "The alchemist did not realize the true essence of the matter. As he sought to discover it, he plunged the unconscious into the obscurity of reality to ignite it. To understand the complexity of the matter, he brought another puzzle— a personal background— into what to say. "The interactions of the alchemists of matter exposed their own mind to them. Jung adds, "I am also inclined to believe that in philosophic theories the true origin of alchemy is to be found less than in individual researchers ' interpretation.... when operating on his chemical experiments the scientist has some psychological perceptions, which appeared to him to be the specific comportement of the chemical method.

The act of projecting is an involuntary and unintended operation, as it is a circuitous road to our consciousness. Jung speculated that "there may have been something in the unconscious of alchemists who had lent themselves to illusions (i.e., appeared to become aware through the energy charge), and that in the alchemical operations they sought a' connection' which would draw them so that they could articulate themselves in some way." The soul, the inherent dignity of the human ego, needed to actualize itself such that the practice of alchemy was developed as a means for its understanding and a symbolic form.

An unconscious, separated and autonomous material lives a personal existence on the subterranean layers of the mind, and, in Jung's terms, is likely "to project themselves automatically if they are approached in some way—that is, when they are pulled in the outside world by anything close to them." "And while the alchemists did not uncover the secret nature of substance," Jung appreciates that "they discovered that of mind, even if they were little conscious of what it implied." Jung's special insight was essential to understand and to demonstrate the true secret significance, sense, and complexity of what the alchemists had found.

Jung says, "But the concept of the unconscious is the sovereignty of the psyche itself, representing not the environment but itself in the play of his photographs, while it uses the illustrative possibilities provided by the receptive universe, such that its photographs are visible." The sensory date of this environment is autonomously selected, manipulated, and designed by the psyche to give form to a certain sort of individual.

In other terms, the unconscious shows itself by its own perceptions into the universe; that is, the unconscious is associated with our perception of existence itself. The unconscious is its own manifestation. What we have to do is accept what is known.

So many people are entranced with their perceptions, persuaded that the way they perceive it is objective. "Practical practice tells us over and over again," Jung states, "that all persistent curiosity over an unseen entity serves as an enticing lure for the unconscious to inject itself through the uncertain essence of the entity and to embrace the resulting impression and the meaning it provides as objective."

Alchemy is an inspiring imaginative type of painting, which deals with our mind's projective instincts to enable us to read, see, and free our visions consciously.

The practice of alchemy is like an elixir of the celestial imagination with psycho-spiritual multi-vitamins and minerals that seeks to cure the collective hysteria that has plagued our world.

SATURN

Alchemy reveals the illumination is veiled in the night, that the greatest gifts are hidden in the distressing, deep depths of the human mind. Jung amplifies the mystery by saying, "The prima materia is' Saturn' and the malefic Saturn is the Devil's abode, or again it is the object most feared, dismissed,' cast out on the lane," set on the dung-hill' and' hidden in the mud.'" The alchemists had a mystical understanding of God, including the light and the shadow, the positive and the bad, an image that became a representation of Christ. "The effort in alchemy is made to symbolically reconcile evil by finding in man himself the spiritual drama of rebirth." This involves a cycle of coming to grips with the unconscious, which is a must even as we encounter its gloom. This conflict compelled the alchemists to locate the prima materia after they had made a significant attempt.

Prima materia was a true numinosum, a sacred, psychically-spiritual material that enabled the alchemists to perceive both the light and the evil of God freely. "In the prima materia, the alchemists dreamt of an" Absolute Grail-like receptacle "that carries, absorbs, incorporates, incarnates, integrates and ultimately liberates both of them, and this, in effect, contributes to the prospect of a true interaction of light and evil, of Heaven and the Spiritual," as Jung notes.

Such divine material formed and combined the representation of God and the Demon, allowing them to recognize deeper the vastness of the Self, the essence of our existence, which comprises both light and darkness.

Symbolically speaking, the prima materia is the lead that affects the destructive parent of Saturn-Chronos. A frail and infirm old guy, the legendary monarch, or "senex," who lost contact with emotions, eros, friendship, imagination, sympathy, and affection, is one of the several icons of prima materia.

This image of the static, man-negative father is representative of the calcification of the psyche, which hangs on to and contributes to power and influence out of fear of its own vulnerability.

The dead old man is a powerful role of the psyche, which has lost its utility and therefore is a barrier to awareness growth and progress. The archetypal character wants liquefied and de-solidified, an alchemical bath in the spiritual healing waters.

There is an alchemical term "solve & coagula," dissolve and coagulate (related to "solution" and "coagulation" alchemical operations).

The Alchemists have both over time and in any moment been dissolving and regenerating aspects of their history and culture in order theoretically to distill, reconstruct and construct something fresh in themselves.

De-establishing, de-literalizing, and de-constructing their history, the alchemists also engaged strongly in their own transitions and development at any moment.

The alchemists considered both analytically and synthetically the nature of their craft because it consisted on one side of isolation, distinction, and examination, and on the other, transformation, strengthening, and incorporation.

Mythologically speaking, Saturn, the twisted patriarch is the jail ruler, who connects us and therefore restricts our independence, while becoming at the same time the ultimate tester and a great purifier. Paradox is the vocabulary of alchemy since it reflects the single perspective, where the obvious opposites are not so distinct.

The dark father's stereotype is linked to the superiority and dominance of others as opposed to being born. The archetypal negative masculinity is obsessed with the oppression of the feminine, with emotion, with spontaneity, with life itself.

Synchronized with the oppressive hierarchy, the broader archetypal cycle is animating occurrences in today's society. Alchemy is a common vision of our ancestors that is now really important to our environment today.

The negative father's model is initiatory, which implies it shows everything to us that we feel best. The image of the negative daughter, seen as a compensating dream cycle, with her willing desire and misuse of control, challenges us to interact with our innate strength, which has been granted by God.

Our true power is a spirit of eros, of relationships, of emotion, of interactions, of love and attachment, which are all elements in the mystical elixir that express the toxic dimension of the coercive image of the negative family.

The dark lord, "Lord Time," must be intransiged and consumed, in linear time, at the detriment of the eternal aspect of our existence, in the bind of Saturn-Chronos. To understand that we perform the mystical cycle of a toxic hegemony on the world stage implies an extension of perception, that we are accessing a metaphysical realm through which time is not "chrono-logical." As we snapped off the magic and rationality of linear time, we wake up to a "Dreamtime" where time is perceived as the circular structure, the middle of which is here and now.

Dreamtime is not dimensional, but spherical, not set, but dynamic, not mechanical but normal. Dissolve the father-time entity; we are inserted into the "synchronic" order by the clock. The synchronous order in which the timing frequency is a fundamental synchronizing factor is a region in limitless contact and interconnection amongst everyone. In the synchronous domain, the microcosm and the macrocosm are synchronous, mirrored mirrors, separate variations of the same, harmonic fractal, underlying. This intertwined fractal represents a remarkable phenomenon that continues indefinitely in infinitely complex and innovative shapes.

The development of the philosopher's stone was similar to the dreamlike existence of the cosmos for the Alchemists. The lucidity of waking dreams is seen as a result of God's continuing universe formation and rebirth. Much like a small piece of a hologram comprises the whole hologram, every individual represents the whole. Jung said, "To the alchemists, the individualization cycle described by the opus was an analogy of the world's creation and the opus itself an analogy of the artistic activity of God.

The co-correspondence of the microcosm and the macrocosm, between the inner and the outer, is the emergence of "symbolic consciousness," which is to understand that this World is not communicating directly, but rather it communicates to us symbolically as a vision. That is the essence of the popular alchemical proverb, "as above, so below."

What occurs in the universe symbolizes what occurs inside us. Alchemy, a true hermetic practice, includes a hermeneutic (interpretation method) of symbols. It is a style of anxiety that takes place in the staff and under the direction of imaginative creativity, where sensory awareness is transfused into living objects, helping the world to perform its revelatory and theophanic purpose (God revealing).

Symbolic knowledge is the very development of consciousness that non-locally dissolves Saturn-Chronos, the negative lord, as a static and set archetypal character in the west, as if pouring water, except in this case, the universe becomes "fluent" and therefore ripened with new possibilities.

A real secret of creation, Alchemy, is the creation into a caring God in the oppressive Hierarchy, the destruction of Nature, the anger of Nature.

Therefore the alchemy is yet another version of the Jesus cycle, a new New Testament, a real "second coming," and this time, the "Incarnation" happens inside and through the unconsciousness of humanity.

Alchemy"... involves a mystery consummated in and around a guy," Jung says. It is as if from now on, the chaos of the creation of Christ is placed in man as his live courier.

As a result, dogma-designed things are familiar and absorbed into subjective experience. "Drafted as instruments of the Incarnating God, we consider ourselves as a culture truly imitating Christ to an ever-growing degree.

But the aim of the Alchemists was, as Jung found out,"... to understand the concept of' Christ' on a stage well beyond pure imitation of him." Christ's imitation of alchemists, to quote Jung, was not' intentional stress after imitation, but the more unintended discovery of reality throughout the holy story.

The fire appears to the adept not in the traditional manner, but in the manner represented by the alchemical legend.

That is the mysterious material that is punished physically and psychologically; that is, the king that lives or is murdered, is dead and buried, and rises again on the third day. And not the expert is doing all that; however, he lives through it, he's being punished, he's going to die and growing again.

Much of this occurs not to the Alchemist himself, but to the' right guy,' whom he thinks is next to him and at the same time the retort... it's the real reality of an individual who engaged in the compensatory contents of the unconscious through his intense exploration of the mysterious and the point of self-sacrifice.

In storing this knowledge alchemically, the alchemists become their own retort, their own hermetically protected box. Participating in the god process, the alchemists formed a relation and thereby became a conduit to the embodiment of the evolving Spirit.

"Opus Christi is passed to the human," Jung continues. He is the carrier of the mystery, which is implicitly prefigured and awaited in alchemy.

Alchemy is like a vision of consciousness itself, which represents and exposes the spiritual cycle of rebirth through which the individual ego has been built up.

THE LAPIS-CHRIST CONNECTION

In and out of the imaginative imaginations of the alchemists, the notion of a philosopher's stone is similar to Christ's Manifestation in our third dimension universe. As Jung contemplates,"... a real understanding of the opus has continued to assimilate or reinforce the orthodoxy.

This is why the text states that Christ was' confrontable and unified' with the stone. "Christ's position in Christianity sought a different realm and structure to function in the stone of the philosopher.

It was as if the stone of the philosophers and Christ were inseparable differentiations within themselves, showing their inseparability when completely distinguished.

The Christian opinion is that we need salvation to give the redemptive task to an independent spiritual entity. In the other side, the alchemists were aware, epochal, progressive, and developmental, that we both participate in the embodiment of the holy being. All viewpoints are valid since they are complementary and unifying parts of a greater whole.

From the alchemical point of view, Jung clarifies,"... the individual takes upon himself the duty of carrying out his redemptive opus and assigns to the anima world soul that is trapped in the matter the state of misery and the consequent need for salvation." Alchemically speaking, it is the mystical material, the actual man, the Self that suffers, is turned into torment and rising again.

That awareness will helpus re-contextualize our perception of pain and reframe it. Instead of connecting individually with our suffering in a manner that restricts, challenges, and enhances them, we are willing to understand that the source of our suffering is transpersonal and archetypal. "Why is the one who is hurting us?"

There is an essential problem as we begin to understand that we, not as a self but as an individual, partake in a divinely funded play of passion.

In our sufferings, we will understand that we are not mere beings apart from the whole of the world through our misery, but instead play roles in a cycle of the godly rebirth that is not the result of our ego but a representation of the Soul.

We witness a symbolic crucifixion, engaging in Christ's agony in order to enjoy his glory. Our pain is our "part" of helping to free the planet spirit, the anima mundi.

This insight changes our viewpoint instantly, pops us out of the selfish mindset of the independent selves, and binds us because we all are in the same plane and on the same side. Compassion is the manifestation of this understanding.

The alchemists were not so much spared by their own work but through their own involvement in the creation of the savior. "For the alchemist," Jung emphasizes, "the one who wants salvation specifically is not the human being, but the god who is lost and latent in the matter. It is only as a secondary concern that he wishes that any profit can be gained by the changed material such as the panacea, medicinacatholica.

He does not focus his attention on his own redemption through the grace of God, but towards saving Christ from the misery of life. By committing himself to the divine research, he gains, but only by the way. "The alchemists represent everything above his small ego, which is a true condition of strength and goodness by venerating the highest meaning. The practice of alchemy is deeply influenced and guided by Christ. An Alchemist claims, "Art has no rivals, but the misguided."

The alchemical god, instead of rising down from heaven, rose up from the sea, from the moon, from the "underworld" itself. According to Jung, the "aspiration" of the alchemists was "the creation of the Deity into man, a man who turns the Deity into the supreme and where the spirit grows out of matter." God becomes born out and through humanity with our aid in the act of being lost in matter. Paradoxically, humanity becomes a living, breathing environment through which the soul becomes evidently imprisoned while at the same time, a tool from which soul materializes through time to be freed.

Spiritually speaking, the release of the spirit in question is not to associate with our thoughts but simply to realize their insubstantial and dreamlike essence and allow them to turn, dissolve, and spontaneously free themselves mercilessly. The complete, self-contained world is like a thought-form. As we understand the contents and points of view of a thinking-form, we are engulfed in the world and represent it in a manner that restricts our artistic independence. Our artistic nature is, therefore, evidently wrapped up in the matter, as we inadvertently used our imaginative force toward ourselves in a manner that connects us. Recognizing the idea and still, the ability of our emotions to construct truth helps us to develop in our ideas rather than making them, recognizing that this moment we never witness but in the artistic imaginations, allows us to change our perception of ourselves alchemically and the whole world by non-local expansion.

Psychologically speaking, Deity, concealed in the matter, reflects the Self symbolically through implicit unity with the ego. This oblivious identification of ego-self, where there is no knowing connection of the ego with the Self but instead an involuntary, compulsive behaving of the mind, pollutes the future unity of opposites, which seems to impede the entire point of the job. Nonetheless, this degradation is nothing other than the raw material itself, from which gold can't be produced. The prima matter is a living organism illusion... our blood. Jung remarks, "The more astute alchemists knew that man himself was the prima materia of the craft."

The Alchemists did not trust in the foundation of the creator, their son of Christ, but in the womb of Mother Nature. For one way, the opus is a work against nature, an "opus contrnaturam" against itself, a task against itself, whatever itself actually wants. The prima matter is an "imperfect body" that requires perfection. The alchemists support nature to accomplish what it can't do. An alchemical proverb says, "Whatsoever nature leaves unfinished, art perfects." Whilst the desire to knowledge resides in nature, and ego is required as a transforming medium for understanding and perfecting this universal impulse inside the unconscious of humanity.

Self-reflection, an act in which we remember ourselves in the mirror of creation, is a re-enactmentof existence and, therefore, a function toward design. The psycho-spiritual imperative of human development overrides the psychological limitations of non-reflective species nature in the moment of self-reflection. Although ego is important for its actualization, reflective consciousness does not exist by the will of the self, but through the observations into individualization, which reside in the Self (the stone of the philosopher). The own desire to think and the urge to respond are the two manifestations of the pillar of the philosopher. In alchemy, we must begin with the stone of the philosopher to render the stone of the philosophy.

The body wants the help and encouragement of the body in a collective opus, whereas the individual and the Self requires the co-operation andcooperation of the individual in order to incarnate in an incarnation. The ego is the offspring of the eternal self, while the selves are the root of the soul. At the same moment, only by ego will the known Self be born in time and space. In this cause, as an addition to naming the "Son of God," Jesus, who symbolizes the Divine, is often named the "Son of Man."

As a consequence of an encounter with the aware human ego, the formless Divine appears as an incarnated, incarnating form; the Self is therefore named the son of man or the son of the philosophers. The practice of alchemists helps God to learn Himself by the particular alchemist.

To borrow an ancient alchemical text, "the stone can be taken to its proper form only by sculpture." Through their holy sculpture, the alchemists actually produced awareness, through finding the stone of the philosopher. Incarnation is unique.

The alchemists had an archetypal vision that it had been God Himself who was trapped in stone, had been drawn into the image, had the doctrine of literalism enthralled, and needed to be rescued from the aid of their alchemists.

And the alchemists, insofar as they did not know that the subject was their own creation, were equally enthralled. As Jung tells us, the alchemists were confronted by the fact "the more they pursued a projection and attributed it to the substance, the further they were removed from their expectations from the psychological source."

If the alchemists did not realize that they were chasing a projection, they escaped them like an ever-rainbow because they tried to grasp the impregnable.

"Alchemists have come to project only the greatest meaning— Nature—into reality," says Jung. If we become ignorant of anything, then we still project something out of ourselves, so it "dreams" through materialization.

Jung clarifies this crucial argument when he states,"… anything unconscious once triggered was formulated into the matter— that is, people from outside approached." Jung adds, "It is not, therefore, unusual that the unconscious occurs in a perceived and symbolic shape since there is no other way it could appear."

Screening affects the receiver of the screening, here the mysterious stone which influences the receiver, which' carries' the predicted material, to render more of the prediction, which serves as evidence for more solidifying the prediction that then simply becomes "printed in stone."

In so far as the alchemists knew that They created their own divinity beyond themselves to accept it within themselves, the alchemists opened the secret to their own sovereignty. When an alchemist understood what he was seeing through his mystery, which he himself was equaling with Jesus, he "would, to quote Jung, be compelled to admit that he had taken Christ's position–or, more precisely, that, thinking himself not as a god, but as a soul, he had taken over the task of the resurrection of not man, but of God. He would also have needed to consider himself, not only as an Approximation to Christ but as Christ as an Ego icon. "In contrast with Heaven, which was the true embodiment of the Sun as the Word rendered flesh, each one of us became a means to bind together and reconcile the paradoxical God, who includes both sun and darkness. We are God's alchemical vessels specially built to combine the opposites inherent in his being.

Conclusion

Importance of Self Improvement for you and your relationship

Since we were young, we had been informed of success in education, emphasis on graduating well, and taking our exams. In schools and colleges,the curriculum was often geared primarily at academic subjects, but what about things such as self-amélioration and personal growth that play an equally important role in human lives?

The value of self-improvement is still overlooked. We either sweep our shortcomings safely under the mat, fail to confront them, or are content to remain oblivious. The reality is—you can't get forever. The more you go, the further you dig a grave when a moment arrives when all these latent feelings come to light and can consume you.

So, what are you going to do? Start to become more aware of yourself, track your feelings, reactions, and actions, and plan to render self-improvement an integral part of your existence.

Even like learning will never cease, self-improvement is the same. The goal would be to reflect at all stages of our lives on ongoing self-development and be stronger iterations of ourselves.

Here are 12 reasons why self-improvement is important irrespective of your age:

1. Increase Self-Awareness

We expend too much energy helping other individuals and addressing their issues. If we had lived that long understanding ourselves, life would have been so much worse. Was it not? Is it not?

The first phase in self-improvement helps you to be more self-confident and well informed. It lets you ask yourself what it is and face the truth, however challenging it might be.

Self-consciousness is a lifelong process–you encounter new encounters and struggles as your life develops, allowing you more mindful of your own attitudes, emotions, and feelings. So it is necessary never to lose contact with yourself to be on the road to self-improvement.

2. Enhance Strengths

Self-improvement helps you to recognize and draw on your own strengths. From partnerships to the job–it is crucial for every aspect of your life to learn your strengths.

It offers you a clear idea of what you are searching for and where you will succeed. It lets you develop and accomplish life goals. After all, only when you realize what you desire can you accomplish what you want. You become more likely to gain achievement and to create a happy, more successful existence by cultivating, playing with your strengths.

3. Overcome Weaknesses

Although recognizing talents is an essential part of self-improvement, the shortcomings are often discussed. Don't feel afraid; see them as development zones. We all have vulnerabilities and strengths that form our personalities. Such imperfections render us different.

The goal of developing yourself will be to reach past the flaws that deter you from reaching grandeur. Consider the shortcomings, figure out where they start, and plan to solve them. It's not convenient, but certainly, it's not impossible. Let your self-improvement quest become a catalyst for any failure and just carry you up.

4. Step out of Comfort Zone

The "hot zone" is a dangerous spot. It definitely feels nice, but it also suggests a plateau, so you will only expect development where there is deflation.

You have to get out of your comfort zone if you want to better yourself. It lets them confront their doubts, do different stuff, take chances, and test themselves. Often you'll experience a different aspect to your nature, but often you'll still struggle. Don't let you weigh down these mistakes. You can never be complacent and too relaxed in familiar spaces because, as you know, life starts beyond your comfort zone.

5. Improve Mental Health

The beneficial impact it has on emotional wellbeing is one of the most significant facets of self-improvement. When you focus on yourself, you grow more and helps you to cope more efficiently with your thoughts and emotions. You continue to recognize why you feel those feelings and how to cope with them over time. Someone who may not know himself and may not work on change has little influence whatsoever of his responses, which can contribute to increased tension and anxiety. The reason is never to be refused.

6. Heal Relationships

As you focus on enhancing yourself, your interaction with others around you naturally changes. For, e.g., if your short-tempered disposition has always been a source of worry in your relationships, you will learn to alleviate your frustration and to relax by actively focusing on that part of your personality. This meaningful shift represents and strengthens personal and professional partnerships.

The secret to resolving disputes and creating successful partnerships starts by focusing inwards and first evolving. Moreover, you are expected to maintain healthier partnerships because you aspire to become a self-sufficient individual and have a good self-image.

7. Motivating Factor

Imagine scaling a mountain–any challenge you encounter motivates you to move higher. The same comparison refers to self-improvement. Each insecurity and limitation you conquer motivates you to keep on changing yourself and to grow.

Motivation and self-improvement go hand in hand. When you see yourself evolving as a human being, you are full of hope and the desire to do better. It is an ongoing process that requires you to sustain your degree of commitment and continue to evolve.

8. Better Decision Making

We have to determine every move of our lives, and every choice has an impact. Moreover, it's not about decision-making as much as it's about getting the choice comfortable.

Effective decision-making skills are a direct product of self-improvement, transparency, self-confidence, and self-assurance. You will take easier, more rational choices when you realize what you want to gain from a scenario and set your targets accordingly.

Do Not Go Yet; One Last Thing To Do

If you enjoyed this book or found it useful, I'd be very grateful if you'd post a short review on Amazon. Your support does make a difference, and I read all the reviews personally so I can get your feedback and make this book even better.

Thanks again for your support!

CPSIA information can be obtained
at www.ICGtesting.com
Printed in the USA
BVHW042328310521
608489BV00016B/2897